Contents

Pathfinder 20

A CILT series for language teachers

Night shift
Ideas and strategies for homework

by David Buckland

and

Mike Short

Other titles in the PATHFINDER series:

Reading for pleasure in a foreign language (Ann Swarbrick)
Communication re-activated: teaching pupils with learning difficulties
　　　　(Bernardette Holmes)
Yes - but will they behave? Managing the interactive classroom
　　　　(Susan Halliwell)
On target - teaching in the target language (Susan Halliwell and Barry Jones)
Bridging the gap: GCSE to 'A' level (John Thorogood and Lid King)
Making the case for languages (Alan Moys and Richard Townsend)
Languages home and away (Alison Taylor)
Being creative (Barry Jones)
Departmental planning and schemes of work (Clive Hurren)
Progressing through the Attainment Targets (Ian Lane)
Continuous assessment and recording (John Thorogood)
Fair enough? Equal opportunities and modern languages (Vee Harris)
Improve your image: the effective use of the OHP
　　　　(Daniel Tierney and Fay Humphreys)
Not bothered? Motivating reluctant language learners in Key Stage 4
　　　　(Jenifer Alison)
Grammar matters (Susan Halliwell)
Differentiation (Anne Convery and Do Coyle)
Drama in the languages classroom (Judith Hamilton and Anne McLeod)

Illustrations by Gill Short

First published 1993
Copyright © 1993 Centre for Information on Language Teaching and Research
ISBN 1 874016 19 4

Cover by Logos Design & Advertising
Printed in Great Britain by Oakdale Printing Co Ltd

Published by Centre for Information on Language Teaching and Research, 20
Bedfordbury, Covent Garden, London WC2N 4LB.

Introduction

The aim of this book is to show homework in a **positive** light by suggesting a range of ideas and approaches that could be both stimulating and useful to language learners of all ages and abilities. Our suggestions are based on the experience of many teachers and we hope that readers will be encouraged to adapt them to meet their own needs.

Our examples are based upon the notion that homework:

- **gives control**
  During the school day pupils have to adapt to the constraints of the timetable and they may frequently be engaged in absorbing tasks when interrupted by the need to move to another lesson. Working at home, however, gives learners more control as they have the choice of when to start working and how long to give to a task.

- **can develop confidence**
  Time spent productively at home, away from the pressures and expectations of teachers and peers, can be a crucial factor in enabling pupils who may lack self-assurance in the classroom to consolidate and extend previously introduced skills and concepts.

- **can promote creativity**
  The classroom may not always be the ideal environment to promote reflection and experimentation. However, by providing additional time to think, plan, prepare and create, homework can unlock the creative potential of pupils of all ages and abilities.

- **can support differentiation by task**
  Learners can be given a choice of tasks, aimed at different levels of difficulty, thereby enabling each member of a class to work at an appropriate level.

- **can support differentiation by outcome**
  Some tasks can be set for the whole class and yet produce widely differing end results. For example, the task of writing about a shopping trip could produce a short, simple, precise piece of work from one pupil, and a more substantial, varied and imaginative contribution from another.

- **can encourage pupil independence**
  By giving pupils opportunities to plan, organise and evaluate their work in the home, we can develop their autonomy. We can also encourage them to

become better, more involved learners by identifying and selecting the homework tasks that are most likely to meet their needs.

- **can support communication between school and parents**
  Most parents support the idea of homework. Although they may argue from time to time that it intrudes on leisure and relaxation, the idea that more homework equals better education is deeply rooted in our culture. Schools therefore value homework as an opportunity to reassure parents that they are promoting self-reliance, independence and good working habits.

- **can provide pragmatic ways of lightening the burden of assessment**
  Few teachers would argue that assessment should be integrated into everyday work. However, there is a risk that the pressures and unpredictability of a busy classroom can divert teachers and pupils from assessment-related tasks, even if they have been carefully planned. All the more reason then to explore the possibility of building additional assessment opportunities into homework.

We strongly believe that homework can provide a unique range of learning opportunities. However, we also acknowledge that it can raise a number of difficult issues. Not all children go home to space, quiet and the opportunity of privacy. Some may have failed to 'grasp the point' in class, so that mistakes risk being reinforced at home. Others may be so conscientious that they spend too much time on homework, becoming tired and stressed.

It is therefore essential that teachers think carefully and creatively about the work that their pupils take home. Wherever possible it should be varied, encouraging and designed with the needs of the individual in mind. It should also relate to a policy which provides clear guidelines on both purpose and practice.

1. Speaking at home

Children normally take home tasks that focus on reading and writing. However, there are effective ways of promoting spoken language as part of homework.

Let's take visual stimuli as our starting point.

Making and using pictograms

Role-play in the modern languages classroom can be repetitive and 'wooden' if the pupil has little input and initial control over the task and its content. Lack of time to reflect and experiment with speech in the classroom can also inhibit the development of the spoken word. Using pictograms to generate speech is a possible homework activity that can help overcome these problems.

Remember, you do not have to be a great artist (or know one!) to use pictograms. However, if all inspiration is lacking you might refer to books such as *1000 pictures for teachers to copy* by Andrew Wright.

This simple pictogram prompt card is relevant to beginners in German.

It could provide the stimulus for helping beginners practise the following set of simple questions:

> *Wie heißt du?*
> *Wo wohnst du?*
> *Wo ist London?*
> *Wie alt bist du?*

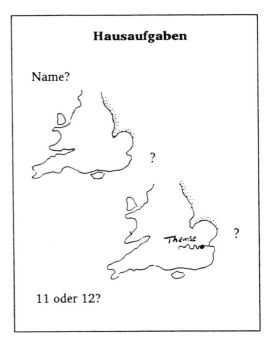

This one is aiming at a prolonged dialogue in French, something like the one below.

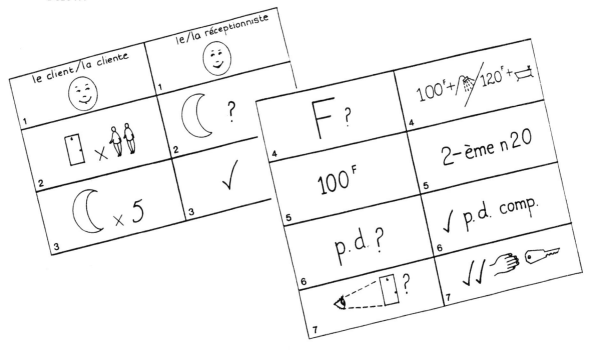

La cliente:	Bonjour.
La réceptionniste:	Bonjour, madame.
La cliente:	Avez-vous une chambre pour deux personnes?
La réceptionniste:	Pour combien de nuits?
La cliente:	Pour cinq nuits.
La réceptionniste:	Oui, madame.
La cliente:	C'est combien?
La réceptionniste:	100 francs avec douche et 120 avec bain.
La cliente:	Je prends la chambre à 100 francs.
La réceptionniste:	Alors, vous avez la chambre numéro 20, au deuxième étage.
La cliente:	Est-ce que le petit déjeuner est compris?
La réceptionniste:	Oui, le petit déjeuner est compris.
La cliente:	Je peux voir la chambre?
La réceptionniste:	Bien sûr. Voici la clef.

Homework based on pictograms such as this can help learners put together and practise phrases and routines that have already been presented in class. It can also provide opportunities for differentiation, since some pupils can produce their own variations and additions, e.g. *Avez-vous une chambre à deux lits avec télévision et vue sur la mer?*, while others could have the target of practising one part only, e.g. that of the *cliente*.

Back in class the homework could be followed up with the pictogram displayed as a transparency on the overhead projector. The teacher could then conceal specific cues, or even all the cues for one of the two parts, thus encouraging the pupils to test their memories as well as reuse the visual information remaining on-screen. Another overhead transparency displaying a further dialogue on the theme could then be presented to reinforce relevant vocabulary and structures. By this time the class should be in a position to respond with speed, accuracy and confidence!

Regular use of pictograms at home to assist oral work can produce excellent results, since over-reliance on the written word to stimulate speech can inhibit the development of confidence and spontaneity. By using pictograms at home pupils can:

- relate to a concept and develop verbal memory without having to grapple with written text;
- internalise key patterns at leisure, thus building a foundation for recycling previously used language in new contexts;
- develop flexibility and creativity, since a symbol can often be 'interpreted' in a number of ways.

As pupils become more familiar with the 'language' and strategies of pictograms, they can be given increasingly challenging and open-ended tasks that will develop useful skills and positive attitudes.

Hausaufgaben

★ Hast du Deutsch gern?

★ Wo liegt Deutschland?

★ Was ist die Hauptstadt von Deutschland?

★ Welche Sprachen spricht man in Deutschland?

Why not give a stimulus, such as the series of questions shown above, as homework for the pupils to draw their own pictograms? This will encourage thinking about meaning, since the pictures will need to be unambiguous and appropriate.

The example above could also serve as a lever against a Eurocentric approach to the teaching of languages, since the question *Welche Sprachen spricht man in Deutschland?* could stimulate an illustration featuring, for example, Turkish as well as German words.

The material resulting from a 'make a pictogram' homework can then be utilised in the classroom to encourage speech. If the prompt has come from the pupils, there is a greater chance that words and structures will be remembered.

Pronouncing the written word
- strategies to promote confidence and independence

Pupils beginning to use a foreign language derive both satisfaction and enjoyment from being able to imitate new sounds. However, they often have difficulty when faced with a need to pronounce what they have read. The following homework tasks are designed to develop the confidence and skills to pronounce the written word.

WORDS ALREADY MET IN PASSING

In this example time is spent at home practising the pronunciation of words that have already been met in a comprehension task in which pupils have listened to a tape, matched person with place and finally added age.

Try to be alert for stimuli that can be recycled as speaking activities. In this case the words in the *Wohnort* column provide an opportunity to practise several sounds (e.g. *ie*, *ei*, *u* and *ü*) that often seem to give young pupils difficulty. The words could be pronounced in front of a mirror at home. Alternatively, their pronunciation could be taught to a trusted friend or adult. Grandparents are normally great listeners!

Name	(Alter)	Wohnort
Jungen		
Rolf	( )	München
Stefan	( )	Saarbrücken
Georg	( )	Freiburg
Thomas	( )	Memmingen
Lutz	( )	Lübeck
Mädchen		
Birgit	( )	Hamburg
Heike	( )	Bremen
Inge	( )	Passau
Gabi	( )	Kiel
Barbara	( )	Stuttgart
Kirsten	( )	Flensburg
Heidi	( )	Trier

WORDS ENCOUNTERED FOR THE FIRST TIME

Give pupils a list of familiar words to pronounce and practise at home. For example, if food and drink is the current French topic, then *petits pois, bol, pain, fruits* and *eau* might well be among the words given.

Match this list with a set of unfamiliar words with similar sound patterns to those already encountered, e.g. *petits pois-bois*; *bol-col*; *pain-main*; *fruits-puits*; *eau-seau*.

Working at home on pronouncing the unfamiliar words gives pupils confidence to experiment away from the attention of the teacher and the class. In the follow-up lesson pupils will be keen to participate and you may be able to capitalise on the patterns of sound that the pupils themselves have discovered, by pointing out a number of 'logical' rules.

Learning by teaching

An interesting way to reinforce new vocabulary and structures is to teach them to someone else. In the following example we can see how Alissa Ozouf, who teaches at Furzehill Middle School in Borehamwood, devised a homework task based on the idea of teaching someone else.

Spend 30 minutes teaching someone how to say the following in French:

a)   their name
b)   their age

c)   where they live
d)   their appearance and personality

If they are quick, maybe you could teach them e) the numbers 1 to 20.

If they are really good, go on to f) the days of the week or g) the months of the year.

To be filled in by the person who was taught

Please would you complete the following questionnaire:

1.   Which areas did you learn? (tick or circle the letters)
     a   b   c   d   e   f   g

2.   How would you rate your teacher on a scale of 1 to 10?

3.   Did you enjoy the activity?

4.   Would you like to learn some more French?

Signature:

Preparation of classwork

For older and/or abler pupils, more extended and open-ended tasks could be set in the form of preparation for further work in class. This could involve:

★ a talk or presentation to give to the class or to a group of peers;
★ a point of view in a debate;
★ interview questions.

To avoid such homeworks being mere script writing sessions, pupils should be made aware that they can only refer to 'skeleton' notes (or maybe no notes at all) during the follow-up.

Learning by heart

Learning speech by heart can be a worthwhile activity if it has a clear purpose. To devote homework to learning a part in a conversation could lead to that conversation being re-enacted in small groups in class. This in turn could lead to a further homework in which pupils are encouraged to make substitutions.

Building blocks

The development of 'building block' phrases as part of homework could be encouraged in the following way.

● Give pupils a small number of short phrases, e.g.:

> *je suis allé*
> *à midi*
> *si vous voulez*
> *mes chaussettes*

- Encourage them to build on as many words and phrases as possible. Again, this is a differentiated task, so that some pupils may do well to produce: *je suis allé / à Bordeaux*, whereas others might manage: *la semaine dernière / je suis allé / en ville / à pied / avec mes copains / pour acheter / des disques / et des vêtements.*

Requiring pupils to 'report back' in class with no access to the written word (other than the original phrase) should ensure that the homework remains focused on speech rather than writing.

Self-assessment

Self-assessment tasks provide an extremely valuable means of developing spoken skills. Set as homework, they enable pupils to take their time to think about and develop their ability to perform a specific task. This in turn promotes a feeling of control and self-awareness which could ultimately lead to the pupil setting his/her own targets.

Pupils are normally very honest when undertaking tasks such as the one shown below. Indeed, they tend to judge themselves too harshly!

Hausaufgaben - Ausspracheübung

Name: _____ Klasse: _____

Ich kann ...

ziemlich gut	✓
gut	✓ ✓
sehr gut	✓ ✓ ✓

	Wort	nachschlagen	aussprechen	jemandem beibringen
1.				
2.				
3.				
4.				
5.				
6.				
7.				
8.				

You can monitor such work with random spot checks in follow-up lessons. If, as is likely, you find that your pupils are approaching such work conscientiously, you will have found an effective way of generating effort and increasing motivation without the penalty of a mountain of marking!

Creative ideas from a textbook

L'île Maurice: un paradis ensoleillé

L'île Maurice est indépendante depuis le 12 mars 1968. On y parle beaucoup de langues: l'anglais (la langue officielle), le français et le créole, et aussi le chinois, l'ourdou et le tamoul.

Le tourisme est la deuxième activité économique de l'île, après la culture de la canne à sucre.

Partez à l'île Maurice
● si vous aimez les activités nautiques, la planche à voile, le ski nautique, la voile, la plongée sous-marine et la pêche
● si vous aimez le soleil, le tennis, les pique-niques et les barbecues sur la plage
● si vous aimez les plats épicés.

Quand partir?
Maurice est située dans l'hémisphère sud. Ses saisons sont donc inversées par rapport à la France. Il fait chaud de novembre à avril; il fait plus frais de mai à octobre. Les températures varient de 13° à 31°. Il est préférable d'éviter janvier et février. C'est la période des cyclones.

À voir absolument!
Le jardin Royal de Pamplemousses. On y trouve toute la flore tropicale, arbres, plantes et fleurs.

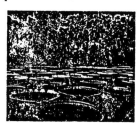

Pour tout renseignement:
Bureau d'Information de l'île Maurice, 41 rue Ibry, 92200 Neuilly. Tél. (1) 47.58.12.40

The above *renseignement touristique*, taken from *Arc-en-ciel 3*, is used in the textbook as a stimulus for reading, listening and speaking activities that could take place in the classroom.

For homework the following speaking activity could also be set:

You have been employed by the Mauritius Tourist Board to make a 20-second publicity clip for use on a local radio station. Make the clip clear, informative and interesting. Remember... it must last 20 seconds!

Such a task could be approached in the following ways:

- select and memorise key phrases from the page:
  e.g.   *Il fait chaud de novembre à avril.*

- adapt key phrases:
  e.g.   *Partez à l'île Maurice pour la flore, le sport et les activités nautiques.*

- create new ideas:
  e.g.   *Pour les vacances de vos rêves, venez à l'île Maurice. C'est jeune, c'est beau, c'est chic!*

In addition...

- it could be produced in pairs and/or on tape (with a musical background?);
- it could be presented in class (teachers must decide whether to allow the support of written prompts) with points awarded for effort, impact and timing;
- it could lead to the creation of posters and other display material.

Above all, the 20-second time rule will ensure that even if pupils write a script at home, the text will have to be practised aloud in order to adapt it to the time permitted.

Such a task, which could be adapted to many other contexts, provides an ideal opportunity for differentiation by outcome. All pupils should be able to reproduce a number of key phrases and there is a great opportunity to be imaginative and creative.

Why not tape it?

All the speaking tasks previously described could be recorded on tape. Giving a pupil the opportunity to record his/her voice could enhance the task in terms of pupil motivation, and at the same time it gives the teacher access to a far greater range of work than would be possible if only a small number of 'samples' were reviewed in class. The teacher can listen to work at her leisure, record her own comments on tape (thus creating an effective and private means of communication) and have at hand a valuable source of evidence for assessment and reporting purposes.

To encourage these practices, schools could include on their equipment lists, alongside the navy blue shorts, atlases, and lab coats:

★ a specified number of good quality C60 tapes (why not recommend a local supplier who could provide a discount?);

★ a simple cassette recorder which will enable recording as well as playback.

If other departments (in particular English) were also keen to promote this policy, the likelihood of it being implemented would be that much greater!

Obviously, such a policy may not achieve 100% success. There may be schools where it would be unrealistic to make such demands, and dependence on the tape recorder as a homework resource could cause constant problems (in any class there will always be some broken machines at any one time).

However, it is not unrealistic to support the use of the tape recorder as a resource to enhance learning at home, providing that tasks set can still be completed in a satisfactory manner in the event of non-availability. In this way the tape recorder can become an asset rather than a management problem.

2. Listening at home

Listening is an aspect of language work in which pupils may be constrained in the classroom by a well-meaning teacher eager for them to pick out specific pieces of information. If this occurs regularly, the received message risks becoming 'Listen for what I want you to hear, not for what you may wish to know or find helpful'. This may eventually lead to an increasingly passive approach to listening and, in certain cases, to a sense of failure.

During a recent in-service training session we heard a teacher recount a lesson in which a year 10 class was working in groups. One group was listening to a tape in French. The teacher's attention was drawn to a child who was making copious notes in a secretive way. When she approached him the piece of paper on which he was writing was hidden away. Was this something illicit? No, not at all! He was simply transcribing the tape into his own version of French phonetics which were, in the written form, totally incomprehensible. However, when she asked him to read back to her what he had written, the result was some very passable French! But why was he so guilty about using his own listening and recording techniques?

With this anecdote in mind, the emphasis of this chapter is on the desirability of **helping pupils acquire their own strategies** for making listening a positive, rewarding and at times open-ended activity, and then to give them opportunities to develop and refine these strategies in the home.

Copying tapes

In order to support listening at home, a department will need to make copies of tapes for pupils to use. It will therefore need to own a fast multi-copier and, if necessary, a bulk eraser. As has already been suggested in Chapter 1, pupils could be encouraged to supply their own good quality tapes or, alternatively, the school could own banks of tapes that could be issued to classes as the need arises. Good management of master tapes is essential if quality is not to be lost, since a copy made from a copy tends to give vastly inferior sound reproduction.

Many new courses allow for multiple copies of taped material to be made within the purchasing institution. Similarly, there is an increasingly wide choice of listening resource packs which also allow for multiple copying. However, to acquire a range of tape-based activities for use in the home does not necessarily mean relying on published materials. Why not use a foreign language assistant or another available native speaker to record tapes?

Different strategies and skills

Home is the ideal place to develop listening competence, since control over time allows for the amount of repetition appropriate to the individual's needs, which in turn can play a major part in developing confidence as well as skills and strategies. Encourage pupils to play a tape as a background to another activity (such as tidying their room!?). Or suggest that they listen closely to a tape at least three times. Once they realise that repetition, although sometimes tedious, can greatly enhance understanding, some may actually wish to listen more!

Alternatively, set tasks that will develop the skills of skimming and scanning. This could involve quite a difficult listening stimulus with a relatively easy task, such as:

★ a *vrai/faux* exercise;
★ picking out specific words and phrases;
★ answering in English (yes... English) questions in either English or the target language.

Possibilities with radio

French radio stations are normally easier to receive than German/Spanish ones. At the time of writing, there is a splendid programme on Radio 5 called *Le Top*. The programme contains items of interest to young people and consists of 'chunks' of French, interspersed with English and lots of music. Pupils could be encouraged to listen to it for fun, to relax and enjoy what they hear. Hopefully this positive broadcasting trend will continue and we will be able to enjoy and use more such programmes in the future. This could do something to counter the countless examples of news broadcasts in which the words of foreign speakers are given voice-overs, as though we have to be protected from the pollution of other languages.

Possibilities with satellite and cable TV

As teachers we should reflect upon the advent of satellite and cable television into more and more homes. It opens up the possibility of more extensive listening, this time supported with visual clues, and brings with it opportunities for increased cultural awareness.

Perhaps pupils who have this form of access to a country, its people and its way of life could be asked, from time to time, to report back to the class on broadcasts that they have found interesting.

Opportunities for feedback

After a listening homework, time can usefully be spent with pupils not only in correcting and marking, but also in talking about the value of listening and, most importantly, how they listen. Do they see words in their head? Or pictures? Does it help them to write down things that they hear? Can they filter information? Does a listening passage begin to get easier the second or third time around? How do they maintain concentration?

Tape exchanges

A useful way of improving listening skills and raising language awareness is to set up an audio (or video) cassette exchange with a partner school abroad. Not, however, with pupils speaking in the target language, but with English pupils speaking English and exchanging their cassette(s) for others made by the partner school in their mother tongue. This exchange of materials could help pupils to become aware of communication strategies involving the need to express themselves clearly and simply to someone with a limited grasp of their language. For example, they will need to be aware that although it may be fun to learn about the slang and dialect of another language, it is not helpful to include on tape expressions that could confuse the recipient.

It is also much more exciting to receive a tape from a partner school in the target language than to hear countless foreign peers expressing themselves in broken English! It is authentic and communicative.

Making a tape to send abroad is a task requiring planning and care. It could be undertaken by pupils working in pairs over more than one homework.

3. Reading at home

Using dictionaries

Among the many positive innovations of the National Curriculum is the emphasis placed upon pupils being taught and encouraged to use dictionaries and reference books. For example, in the area of the Programmes of Study directed at developing the ability to learn independently, it is stated that pupils should have regular opportunities to use a range of reference materials and resources (e.g. glossaries, exercise books, textbooks, bilingual and monolingual dictionaries, indexes and encyclopaedias).

To many this might seem a worthwhile yet unattainable ideal as, for example, they observe sixth formers struggling to make productive use of dictionaries. Certainly the majority of pupils need to spend time in the classroom learning and then practising dictionary skills. But it will be time well spent if it results in pupils becoming increasingly independent of the teacher and consequently increasingly capable of reaching higher levels of attainment. Time spent at home consolidating these skills would therefore seem equally worthwhile.

Since it is imperative for pupils to have access to the same dictionary in order to save unnecessary wastage of time and effort, should not language departments specify as part of the school equipment list a simple and manageable dictionary, for example the *Collins Gem*, for use in their lessons and at home? A whole-school policy that supports appropriate use of dictionaries as early as year 7 will bear fruit in later years.

Having been taught in the classroom to use the 'target language into English' section of a dictionary, pupils can now practise dictionary skills at home. For example:

> Trouvez:
> ★ le mot 'pantalon'
> ★ cinq adjectifs qui commencent par 'b'
> ★ cinq mots qui commencent par 'i' et qui sont les mêmes en anglais (e.g. intelligent, etc)

Dictionaries can also be used in an interesting way to support working from English to the target language. For example, to ask a pupil to find the meaning of the word 'cup' (as a trophy, rather than as a receptacle for tea), or the meaning of 'coat' (as in coat of paint) can be an effective way of raising language awareness while at the same time emphasising the need to look closely at all the information that a dictionary may provide in relation to a particular word.

A range of such words could be distributed as homework within groups of pupils.

For example:

> - the class is split into groups of four pupils;
> - pupil 1 in each group is given a set of words, e.g. train (on a dress), file (for papers), shoe (for a horse), cricket (the insect), swing (in a playground), head (as in leader) and boot (for a car);
> - pupils 2-4 are given similar lists;
> - in class the groups come together; each pupil is given the opportunity of reporting back to the others on the words that he/she was asked to find, the strategies that were used and the information that was recorded.

A further homework could be to ask pupils to make similar lists of their own to set for others. Successful completion of such a task could be identified as an important 'landmark' in the development of language awareness.

Building a glossary

Such a homework leads naturally to the creation of a pupil glossary. This should be geared to the level, maturity and ability of the pupil. It is also a task that can be repeated over a sustained period of time. We have found paradoxically that setting a minimum number of words to be looked up and recorded serves as a great **motivator**. Homework can all too often be not only uninspiring but also too difficult and too long, and this can lead to poor performance. However, by perverse human psychology, we have found that when set a minimum homework requirement, pupils seem to produce far more than they are 'legally' bound to!

Finding new words

Another way of bringing this type of homework back into the classroom is to set a 'Wort der Woche' (word of the week). This should be set as an 'extra' homework, whereby a single pupil in the class has the additional task of looking up a word to be displayed in the classroom. The word could be a free choice for the pupil - for sheer fun - or linked to a topic or area of experience currently being taught and practised in the classroom. For eager and more able or older pupils this could become the 'Satz der Woche' (phrase of the week).

Imaginative approaches to reading a story

Some coursebooks include a running story that recurs at regular intervals, for example *Das Nibelungenlied* in *Deutsch Heute Neue Ausgabe*. Such a story can be used for extensive reading, where the prime aims are gist understanding and enjoyment. Pupils can also be asked to examine more closely the written word. Let's take the following episode of *Das Nibelungenlied* as a starting point and brainstorm ways in which it could be exploited at home without engaging the teacher in an onerous amount of preparation.

Das Nibelungenlied

Aber etwas hat Siegfried getroffen. Er hat aber nichts gesehen und er hat nichts gehört! Wer war das?

1

Au!! Wer war das? Grrr! Wer ist da?

2   Dann hat Siegfried das Ding gefaßt und geschüttelt und...da stand Alberich der Zwerg, Freund des Königs Nibelung. Alberich hatte eine Zaubermütze getragen. Die Zaubermütze machte ihn unsichtbar. Im Kampf war die Zaubermütze ihm vom Kopf gefallen.

Was ist das? Wo bist du?

3   *Alberich. Gib mir diese Mütze! Komm, gib sie mir. Sonst haue ich dir den Kopf ab.*

Ach weh! Muß ich?

4

Jetzt bin ich König der Nibelungen. Ich bin euer König. Ihr seid alle in meinem Dienst.

Ich nehme etwas Gold und die Zaubermütze mit nach Hause.

5   Siegfried ist in Xanten angekommen. Er hatte viele Soldaten und viel Gold.

Tag, Papi! Tag, Mami! Ich bin König der Nibelungen und habe auch viel Gold. Ich habe auch diese komische Zaubermütze bekommen.

Du kommst zu spät für das Mittagessen.

6   *Ach Sigi! Wie nett. Möchtest du einen Kaffee mit einem Stück Kuchen? Wir haben Pflaumenkuchen. Sehr lecker.*

7   Die drei Leute sind also ins Schloß gegangen, wo sie Kaffee getrunken und Kuchen mit Sahne gegessen haben. Siegfried war sehr zufrieden. Er war jetzt König der Niederlande, König der Nibelungen und hatte viel Gold und viele Soldaten.

Sigi, möchtest du auch König der Niederlande sein?

OK. Ja. Das wäre ganz fein.

getroffen *struck*   2 Ding *thing* gefaßt *grasped* geschüttelt *shaken* Zaubermütze *magic cap*
unsichtbar *invisible* Kopf *head*   3 sonst *otherwise* haue...ab *chop off*   4 Dienst *service*
6 Kuchen *cake* Pflaumenkuchen *plum cake* lecker *tasty*   7 Schloß *castle* Sahne *cream*

Pupils could:

- read the episode for understanding and fun;
- make a list of words that are the same or similar to English words;
- look up the nouns at the bottom of the page for gender;
- transpose the third person singular to the first person;
- make a list of what they consider to be the key words and talk about them next day in class;
- look up any words not understood;
- write a follow-up (in English?);
- make a list of opposites from the text, e.g.:
  König - Königin
  Kampf - Friede
  spät - früh
- translate or paraphrase the episode for a non-German speaker;
- put a part of the episode into the negative.

Such homeworks do not necessarily rely upon items of vocabulary, structure or areas of experience having been previously introduced. They can be taken 'off the shelf' and used to support independent choice and differentiation by outcome.

Setting questions

Another way to encourage reading at home is to give the pupils a passage and then ask them to set the questions (in the target language or in English) and mark-scheme for the text as a reading comprehension.

Strategies to support reading for information and pleasure

The home environment has the potential to support extensive reading. Many children arrive at secondary school having benefited from a regular programme of home reading in the primary phase, and reading homeworks can be the norm in other subjects. Pupils should therefore be familiar with the idea of reading for information and pleasure at home, and could well possess skills and strategies that could be reapplied in the context of a foreign language.

However, it is also true that many if not most pupils spend far more time in front of the television than reading a book. Perhaps we can provide a counterbalancing influence. In the Pathfinder, *Reading for pleasure in a foreign language*, Ann Swarbrick lists many positive ways in which pupils can find success and enjoyment in reading. Many of her ideas can be extended to the home.

Commercially available reading schemes, such as *Bibliobus*, *Lire davantage* and *Lesekiste*, could be introduced in the classroom and in the school library, and could then be used as the core of a homework reading scheme.

There may well be some readers whose subject matter can provide the platform for other tasks that could be undertaken in the home. For example, the reader *Lire entre les lignes* (Bibliobus, Collection C) could lead to further work on language and content of advertisements. Material such as shown below, supported by the comments within the reader itself, could form the starting point for a review of advertisements in the French speaking press. This could lead to further homework in which pupils create their own portfolio of material taken from newspapers and magazines. Alternatively, they could be encouraged to create and present their own advertisements for others to comment on.

Newspapers and magazines

Authentik is a series of packages, consisting of a 20-page newspaper and a 60-minute cassette, in German, Spanish and French. Published five times a year,

Authentik contains a wealth of material, based on current events and issues, which will stimulate and interest the learner. The possibilities of using such material to support both reading and listening for interest and pleasure in the home are many. However, teachers may not always have the time to keep up with these materials and monitor their students' reading. They may also wish to develop their students' independent study skills. With this in mind, *Authentik* also publish a learner's supplement containing transcripts, activities and exercises, as well as a user's guide that makes practical suggestions as to how the learner could organise his or her own learning.

Many schools subscribe to the wide range of magazines produced by Mary Glasgow Publications and Accent Educational Publishers, all of which encourage reading both in the classroom and at home. *Okapi* (an authentic publication for French teenagers) has also proved itself excellent and stimulating.

Authentic German magazines published for teenagers can prove to be something of a 'strong brew' with their frankness and teenage sexual content. Some teachers, pupils and parents may find them too strong. Nevertheless, passages from the magazines may be given to pupils for non-controversial consumption within an extensive reading programme.

Providing appropriate texts

In order to increase opportunities for reading for pleasure at home, departments could gradually build up a bank of texts. This could consist of:

★ Authentic material obtained in the appropriate country - at last you can do something with all those tourist office leaflets, comics and periodicals you brought back from your trip abroad two years ago!
★ Articles taken from magazines obtainable in this country. Once your copy of *Authentik* is out of date, cut it up!
★ Reading materials from different coursebooks. For example, you may not be using *Arc-en-ciel 3* in your school, but an investment in half a dozen copies of the pupil's book could provide you with a large range of texts (including poems and comic strips) covering interesting themes such as art, space, healthy eating, juvenile crime, fashion and the environment.

It could be supported by a simple method of classification, for example:

★ a 'five star' system denoting degree of difficulty;
★ an indication of the subject matter or theme.

Such a system enables pupils to select accessible, interesting and challenging texts to enjoy at home. A manageable system for reporting back would ensure that work was monitored and would, at the same time, provide helpful previews for future readers.

Letting the computer do the work

The advent of CD-ROM technology can provide further opportunities for learners to:

- select appropriate texts from a large bank;
- print them out;
- take them home to read.

Autolire, a CD-ROM package produced by Collins, has been designed for this purpose. It is a compact disk containing several hundred texts supported by sound recording, images and an electronic dictionary. As a result of government funding nearly all secondary schools in England now own at least one CD-ROM drive that can be connected to a computer in order to 'read' CD-ROM disks. In many schools the CD-ROM machine is to be found in the library, thereby providing access to learners from any curriculum area. *Autolire* can be 'searched' independently by the learner in order to obtain texts according to interest and level of ability. Of course the text can be read while the learner is sitting at the screen, but it can also be printed out and taken away. It can even be downloaded on to a floppy disk, taken to another computer, imported into a word processor and then edited or transformed for the learner's own use!

4. Writing at home

For many pupils written homeworks are the norm, despite the fact that writing in a foreign language frequently presents difficulties, even when supported and monitored by the teacher in the classroom. Small wonder then that written work produced at home is not always successful and rewarding.

'Traditional' approaches to written homework

Homework in a foreign language frequently takes the form of simple exercises designed to consolidate a specific aspect of grammar or vocabulary. These exercises have their place, but since they are unlikely to be intrinsically motivating, their importance and relevance need to be justified before the homework and reinforced afterwards.

Alternatively, pupils can be asked to complete writing tasks with more open-ended outcomes - perhaps a description or a short narrative. However, the writer may lack the skills or techniques to perform such a task successfully or his/her motivation to succeed may be reduced if the subject matter is mundane and lacking in communicative purpose.

Finding new opportunities

Modern languages departments that periodically review their work may well conclude that writing should be communicative, creative, accurate and, above all, fun. Perhaps there are ways in which the opportunity to write reflectively away from the busy classroom can support these aims.

Poetry

The Cambridgeshire Poetry Writing Project has shown that with high expectations, appropriate support, a potential audience and above all, time, children with limited vocabulary and grammar can produce original, forceful and amusing work, as is shown in the example below.

> *Il y a des gens qui disent que je suis trop grosse.*
> *Il y a des autres qui disent que je suis trop maigre.*
> *Il y a des gens qui disent que je suis trop grande.*
> *Il y a des gens qui disent que je suis trop petite.*
> *Je dis que je suis bien!*

Interestingly, the teachers responsible for the project make the following point in their *Ideas for teachers* booklet:

It takes time to write a good poem. You might consider pupils writing and re-drafting over a series of lessons, however, some teachers taking part in the last project found that their classes were motivated to write poems at home.

Presenting text

Since the teacher cannot be present to support the pupil writing at home, it makes sense to set only small amounts of writing - small, but aiming for originality and quality in presentation. This need not just take the form of a chart, poster or diagram; it could also involve designing with words or phrases themselves, as demonstrated below.

Le Soleil

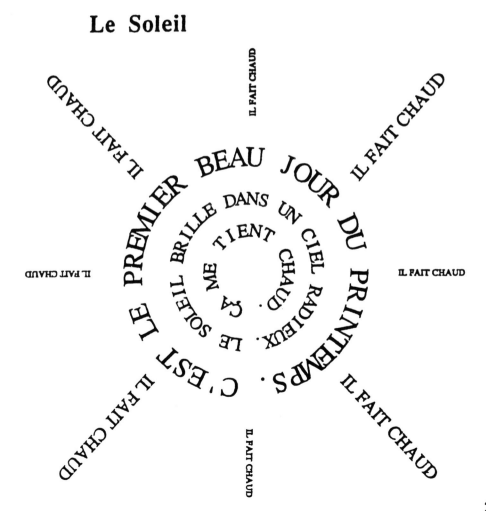

o n

b   d   r e

e   i   t   b   d i

le ballon   r   t e   o n   t

chaque	euqahc
matin	nitam
je	ej
me	em
regarde	edrager
dans	snad
le	el
miroir	riorim

Ich habe mir das Bein ge   br   o   che   n

t
f
u
L
e
i
d
n
i
h
c
o
h
t
g
e
i
l
Der Drachen f

Of course, those that set such homeworks run the risk that some pupils may lack the imagination to complete the task effectively; but for many there will be the time to discover that writing in a foreign language can be fun as well as of interest to an audience.

Writing with a computer

The essential difference between word processing and writing (or typing) is that a word processed text need never be a final product. If saved to disk, it is always capable of being revised, improved or updated.

The implications of this new writing process should not be underestimated by teachers who are all too aware that the average learner's attempts at writing are normally characterised by failure. However, it is possible to reverse negative outcomes, transform attitudes and encourage success by word processing techniques which allow learners to take part in an active and, if possible, collaborative process evolving from initial rough draft, through teacher, peer or self-directed editing, to the final perfect copy. With word processing the correction of errors can take on a positive aspect since a preliminary print-out can easily be edited and upgraded. Writers gain the confidence to experiment as well as the motivation to express themselves and to take an active interest in the language they are using.

Since many homes now possess a computer, it is worthwhile encouraging pupils to take advantage of the potential support it can provide. Word processing software exists for the majority of computers that are mainly bought for the purpose of playing games. Writing produced with this software can frequently be saved on disk as a plain text file and transferred to the school's own machines. Even if this is not possible, and even if foreign accents cannot be created, the process experienced by the writer should still be both positive and rewarding.

The National Curriculum requires all pupils to have the opportunity to draft and redraft texts. What more natural way to do this than with a word processor? And what more helpful environment than the home, where pressures of time are likely to be minimised?

Of course, not all pupils will have access to a word processor. However, it may be possible to arrange for groups of two or three to work together at the home of the lucky owner. Alternatively, opportunities may be found to use the school's own equipment at lunchtime or after school. A school's IT policy should include positive approaches to the use of computers in the home. Supported by a whole-school approach, effective use of this powerful resource is becoming increasingly possible.

Getting prepared

If pupils are expected to write at home, it is essential that the teacher chooses an interesting task. Equally, there should be sufficient preparation in class time to ensure that pupils are clear about the task and have the necessary knowledge and skills to complete it. It may also be desirable to have begun the task in class, so that confidence can be built and ideas can be clarified and shared. This preparation could take the form of oral work - it need not necessarily involve the pupil in writing. Below is an example...

In order to develop work on the perfect tense, a teacher set a homework in which pupils were to imagine themselves feeling depressed. They were then to write up to fifteen things that had happened to bring on the depression. Time was allowed in class for pupils to work in small groups with the purpose of making up some short sentences. No writing was allowed and no words could be looked up. Results included:
- *Je me suis levée tard.*
- *J'ai manqué l'autobus.*
- *J'ai perdu mon livre de français.*
and these were written on the blackboard.

Time was then given to each group to make up two or three more sentences. This time they were allowed to look up words and ask up to two questions, but they were still not allowed to write. The results became more sophisticated, for example:
- *Ma mère m'a grondée.*
- *Mon chien m'a mordue.*
- *Arsenal a perdu contre Tottenham.*
- *La télé est tombée en panne.*
- *Je me suis disputé avec mon meilleur ami.*
and these were also recorded for pupils to see.

Pupils were then given more time to work alone or in groups discussing their strategies for the homework. Only in the last three minutes of the lesson, with the sentences now removed from the blackboard, were they allowed to begin writing. At this point some pupils began to write everything that they could remember from the lesson, whereas others preferred to 'do their own thing'. This was the intention of the teacher. Results were interesting, amusing and original. They also contained a high level of accuracy, since everyone seemed to genuinely value what was being done. The homework had not been an afterthought when the bell went. It had been the final part of a carefully structured lesson plan.

# 5.	Setting and recycling homework

Departmental planning

Homework should be planned as part of a lesson continuum, and not given as an afterthought. Departments will therefore need to plan and share homeworks as part of each unit of work. This will ensure:

★	a consistency of approach across a year group;
★	a bank of relevant tasks produced collaboratively, so that workload is shared;
★	a focus for discussion about homework, its content and purpose.

Setting homework to support assessment

Homework can be set with the purpose of supporting assessment within the National Curriculum. For example, listening tasks, completed at home and without the pressures of time, could enable pupils to fulfil any number of the statements of attainment in Attainment Target 1 (listening), such as:

5a)	*understand and respond to sequences of spoken language which include familiar words, phrases and material from different contexts.*

7b)	*summarise the gist and report specific information or details from messages, news items and narratives.*

Similarly, there could be opportunities to rehearse or record speech with a view to achievement in Attainment Target 2 (speaking), for example:

3c)	*express feelings, likes and dislikes in simple terms.*

7c)	*give clear instructions to explain how something is done.*

In Attainment Target 3 (reading), pupils might:

2b)	*find out the meanings of new words by referring to exercise books, textbooks or glossaries.*

6b)	*choose reading material and read independently from a range of suggested texts.*

Homework could also address assessment objectives in Attainment Target 4 (writing), such as:

4b)   *adapt a simple text by substituting individual words or set phrases.*

8a)   *write a short non-factual text, responding to and developing the content of something read, seen or heard.*

To assist assessment, teachers could have a bank of homework assignments relating to different attainment targets and levels. Pupils could access them when ready and return to them at a later time if they felt the need for further reinforcement or practice. In this way, independent and differentiated learning becomes increasingly possible, eliminating 'whole-class' homework which is aimed at the middle of the ability range and therefore, by definition, too difficult for some and not sufficiently challenging for others.

We need to be aware that National Curriculum assessment need not take place under test conditions. Instead, assessment should be planned into normal work, and this should include homework.

Teachers may be concerned that they cannot directly monitor work set at home. However, they should be aware that coursework undertaken at home is a common feature of assessment in many subjects. If a piece of work is accompanied by a clear description of the task and its context, and backed up with teacher comments and notes, there is every reason to suppose that it could be used to support assessment. Trust between teacher and pupil and respect for the teacher's professional judgement are the cornerstones of continuous assessment. There is no reason why these principles cannot be applied to homework.

Pupil planning

It should be possible, from time to time, for pupils to participate in the process of planning and setting appropriate homework.

Time spent doing this will help raise awareness of:
★ the content of a unit of work;
★ the learning objectives of the unit;
★ a range of learning strategies.

Here are three examples of homework successfully planned and negotiated by pupils. The ideas suggested relate to many of the ideas included in earlier chapters.

EXAMPLE 1 - BRAINSTORMING AND CHOOSING

A unit of work on food and drink includes the following objectives:

★ know vocabulary to deal with mealtimes;
★ be able to ask for things at table;
★ be able to offer things at table;
★ be able to ask to help when preparing/clearing up.

Pupils brainstorm possible homeworks that could help achieve these objectives. This produces a range of differentiated tasks, covering a variety of skills and levels, from which pupils can choose according to their needs.

Among these tasks (all of which exemplify ideas outlined earlier in this book) are:

Speaking

- Practise asking and offering during mealtimes at home. Report back to the class on how easy it was to do and how members of the family reacted.
- Have a friend round for a meal. Try to speak in the foreign language.
- Teach a parent/guardian some of the key content of the unit. Then help them practise at mealtimes.
- Set a target for self-assessment. This could include being able to:
  - ask to do two things to help before a meal;
  - ask to do two things to help after a meal;
  - offer four things to others at table;
  - ask for four things at table.
- Make a taped mealtime conversation at home.
- Make a pictogram of a mealtime dialogue.

Listening

- The teacher (or pupil, or language assistant) makes a 'key phrase' tape which is copied and used at home for listening and speaking practice.

Reading

- Look up at least six items of vocabulary that you don't yet know, for example:
    - place mat;   - dish;
    - table spoon;   - grapefruit.

  Practice pronouncing these new words and put them into your glossary.

Writing

- Write a poem describing a fridge containing old, forgotten items of food and drink, for example:

    Voici une tomate
    Elle est grise et vieille
    Elle a trois mois
    Derrière le yaourt
    Il y a une carotte
    Comme le nez d'une sorcière

- You are working for an estate agent that has sold a house in France to a client. Make a list, in French, of all the cutlery, crockery and tableware that the client will have to buy at the local hypermarket for the dining room. There are five people in the family.

If this approach to negotiated homework is encouraged in the early stages of language learning, it could help pupils to work with increasing confidence and independence in later years. This in turn will help them achieve higher levels of attainment than would otherwise have been possible.

EXAMPLE 2 - CHOOSING AND RECORDING

In this example a range of differentiated tasks is provided for consolidation and/or extension to support a unit of work. The tasks were not difficult to create. Some were designed by the teacher, but the majority refer back to activities in the pupils' coursebook.

The tasks, which are coded, cover the four skills (L, S, R, W) and are graded by a star system denoting three levels of difficulty. They are incorporated in a whole-class 'study map' (see below) that could be devised in any language.

Study map

Language: French   **Work unit: shopping**

	*	**	***
L	SHL1		SHL2
S	SHS1 SHS2	SHS3	SHS4
R		SHR1	SHR2 SHR3
W	SHW1	SHW2	

Pupils select coded tasks from the study map. The tasks are explained in full on work cards. It is intended that work on these tasks should take place over a period of three lessons and one homework. There is therefore an expectation that pupils will plan for homework by thinking ahead and making appropriate choices.

All work completed, including homework, is recorded on a work plan which complements the study map. The teacher monitors what is going on by occasional spot checks.

Work plan

Name: Tony Morley   **Form:** 8 DY

Language: _____   **Work unit:** SHOPPING

Date	Task ref.	Level	Skill	Class/home	Score
3/6/93	SHS2	*	S	Class	8
5/6/93	SHR1	* *	R	Home	7
5/6/93 - 6/6/93	SHW1	*	W	Home and class	1 ☺

EXAMPLE 3 -
MORE OPEN CHOICE, MORE OPPORTUNITIES FOR INDEPENDENCE

In the CILT publication *Letting go - taking hold*, Bridget Barling of Broomfield School, Southgate, describes how she created a list of types of homework from which pupils could make their own choices. The list consisted of tasks such as:

★ *apprendre des mots;*
★ *faire un exercice de* Tricolore *à la page ...;*
★ *enregistrer ma voix sur cassette;*
★ *enregistrer une conversation (au téléphone,dans un magasin, à l'hôtel etc);*

★ *écrire mon journal;*
★ *faire un 'mots cachés';*
★ *écrire une conversation;*
★ *faire un dessin animé avec paroles.*

Bridget comments:

> *I must admit that it did seem like a miracle in the beginning. Pupils were enthusiastic, choosing their preferred task (some of them spending hours on their work). For me, the most exciting homeworks that came back were conversations on tapes with brothers, sisters, parents, aunts, uncles, friends. There were those, of course, who went for the* mots cachés *every time (until directed). But it worked.*

Recycling homework

Examples of homework could be saved and recycled to show to other classes. This stock of good models would help ensure that pupils are clear about what is to be done and that they have a high standard to emulate.

Good homework could also be made available for instant review and evaluation by the class. For example, a piece of interesting writing could be photocopied onto an overhead transparency and displayed for the class to comment on.

This would ensure that:
• homework is reviewed in a positive manner;
• pupils participate in the review;
• the natural interest that pupils have in each other's work is exploited.

In addition, it should be noted that the focus of the overhead projector is the ideal way of securing the attention of the whole class. Parts of an overhead transparency can be hidden or revealed, according to need. A transparency can also be written on, if necessary, and it is far less costly and easier to store than 30 photocopied sheets! In the CILT publication *Improve your image*, Daniel Tierney and Fay Humphreys suggest a whole range of creative uses of the OHP.

6.   Moving forward

Departmental policy

Modern languages departments will benefit from having a homework policy. A clear policy is an agent for change. Without one, departments will find it difficult to work as a team to improve the quality and variety of homework.

As with all policies, it will only be effective if 'owned' by the whole department. This means that if an initial draft is created by one or two teachers, it will need to be referred to the whole department for discussion and amendment before finally being accepted.

The policy could address the following areas:

★ the purpose of homework;
★ links with whole-school homework policy;
★ links with departmental marking policy;
★ examples of successful homework;
★ use of the homework diary as a means of communication with parents and the form teacher;
★ use of resources, both belonging to the school and in the home;
★ strategies for monitoring the effectiveness of the policy;
★ strategies for evaluating and developing the policy.

Developing and implementing the policy

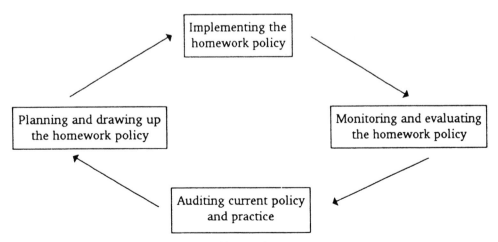

Above is a diagram of a 'classic' policy cycle.

Such a diagram could be used in relation to other policies, for example marking, assessment or use of the target language. Policy development is relevant to individual teachers, groups of teachers and, most important of all, whole departments.

To use the diagram...

- decide on which of the four boxes is most appropriate as your starting point;
- begin and continue the cycle by following the arrows from one stage to the next.

The tasks set out below can be used to support this process.

Tasks for departments

This Pathfinder has suggested a range of homework activities that will make learning and using a modern foreign language at home more creative and enjoyable.

This aim is surely relevant to one of the major issues emerging from the National Curriculum, namely that departments will manage their time and resources in a more organised and effective manner, so that both pupils and teachers may collectively benefit. The days of the gifted but isolated amateur seem to be numbered!

With this in mind, here is a series of tasks for teachers. They do not necessarily have to be undertaken in the order shown, but the greatest good will come if departments work at them together with the purpose of achieving an agreed and unified outcome. *Viel Glück!*

1 Review the foreign language homework set for one class over a half-term period. What was the range of skills required and was differentiation built into the homework tasks? Were all the homeworks taken from the coursebook, or were they created by the teacher? If so, were these homework ideas shared across the whole year group?

2 Monitor the amount and quality of homework set for the whole year group over the same half-term period. According to the information collected, how can the modern languages department improve the quality (and quantity?) of homework given to its pupils?

3 Take **one** unit of work and brainstorm homework activities. Try to ensure that:

- the whole ability range is covered;
- the four skills are addressed, either discretely or in combination;
- setting and marking do not involve onerous amounts of work.

4 Involve pupils in the setting and marking of homework as follows:

- Set a choice of homework tasks based on one unit of work. Take time in the next lesson to discuss the pupils' choices. Does what they say throw any light on your department's approach to homework?
- For one homework task ask a year 8 class to set homework either for peers or for a year 7 class.

5 Involve colleagues from other departments in your discussions. Can any of their ideas be adapted to your needs?

6 Invite a member of senior management to a meeting where homework is on the agenda. He/she could prove to be a useful ally!

Monitoring your review

A 'homework review checklist' is featured on page 37. It is intended to serve as a simple and manageable document that will support departments wishing to conduct a review of any of the six tasks given above.

Homework review checklist

Task review:_____   Lead teacher:_____

Review started:_____   Class/Year:_____

Review finished:_____   Language(s):_____

1. Was the whole department involved in the task?

   ☐ Yes   ☐ No

   If not, why not?

   _____

   _____

2. List the main positive areas that have emerged, e.g. creative homework,
   collaborative work. _____

   _____

   _____

3. List - if necessary! - areas that may give cause for concern, e.g. repetitive
   homework, inconsistency across the department in variety and type of
   homework set. _____

   _____

   _____

4. Has there been an improvement in pupil response to

   ☐ homework?_____

   _____

   ☐ classwork? _____

   _____

   _____

References

Methodology and resources

Cambridgeshire Modern Languages Poetry Writing Project - Ideas for teachers (Cambridgeshire County Council Education Service)

Page B, ed, *Letting go - taking hold: a guide to independent language learning by teachers for teachers* (CILT, 1992)

Swarbrick A, *Reading for pleasure in a foreign language* (CILT, 1992)

Tierney D and F Humphreys, *Improve your image: the effective use of the OHP* (CILT, 1992)

Wright A, *1000 pictures for teachers to copy*, (Collins ELT, 1984)

Coursebooks

Arc-en-Ciel (Mary Glasgow Publications)

Deutsch Heute Neue Ausgabe (Nelson)

Magazines

Language magazines in French, German and Spanish available from:
    Mary Glasgow Publications
    Accent Educational Publishers
    Authentik Language Learning Resources

Okapi
    published fortnightly by Bayard Presse Jeune
    available on subscription from European Schoolbooks

Readers

Autolire (Collins Educational)

Bibliobus (Mary Glasgow Publications)

Lesekiste (Mary Glasgow Publications)

Lire davantage (Heineman Educational)

A world of words
and
Another world of words
(anthologies of poems in foreign languages written by children in Cambridgeshire schools)

Radio programmes

Le Top, with Marc et La Mèche
Currently on Saturday, 7.30 - 8.30 pm:
BBC Radio 5

National Curriculum documentation

Modern Foreign Languages for ages 11-16
(October 1990)

Modern Foreign Languages in the National Curriculum
(November 1991)